THE COUNTRY PRESERVES

Jams & Jellies,
Chutneys, Pickles,
Marmalades and Mincemeat

compiled by
Carol Wilson

with illustrations by
Helen Allingham RWS

SALMON

Index

Cover pictures: *front:* The Apple Orchard *back:* Hedgerow Harvest by Beringer Benger
title page: At Granny's Door

Copyright, Printed and Published by J. Salmon Ltd., Sevenoaks, England ©

Jams and Jellies

All fruit for jam making must be dry, fresh and not quite ripe. To tell when setting point has been reached, remove the pan from the heat and put a little jam on a chilled saucer. As it cools the jam should begin to set, will wrinkle slightly and remain in two separate parts when you draw your finger through it; a sugar thermometer will read 220°F/110°C. Jars must be clean and warm before filling; fill to the brim to allow for shrinkage. Wash the jars in hot soapy water, rinse and put in a low oven to dry and become warm. Stand on folded newspaper to prevent cracking when the hot jam or jelly is poured in. For jellies you will need a jelly bag (from cookware shops) which should be scalded by pouring boiling water through it so the fruit juices do not soak into it. Do not squeeze the bag to speed up the process or the jelly will be cloudy.

Fruit Curds and Butters. Fruit curds are made with butter and eggs and thus have a short shelf-life of just a few weeks. Fruit butters also have a short shelf-life as they do not contain such a high proportion of sugar to fruit as jams. Their name comes from their soft, smooth, butter-like consistency. Fruit butters are not covered with waxed discs but with airtight metal or plastic lids. Store both curds and butters in a cool, dark place.

Apple, Pear and Quince Jam

This old country recipe is useful as it only requires limited quantities of hard, cooking pears and of quinces, which are combined with the more easily obtained cooking apples.

2 lbs cooking apples	Rind and juice of a lemon
2 lbs cooking pears	6 lbs sugar
1½-2 lbs quinces	2 pints water

Wash the fruit and rub away the grey down from the quinces. Peel and core the fruit and cut into pieces. Retain the peel and cores and tie loosely in a piece of muslin together with the lemon rind. Put the fruit, muslin bag and water into a large pan, bring to the boil and simmer gently until all the fruit is completely tender. Squeeze out the muslin bag into the pan to extract all the juice and discard. Add the sugar to the pan, stirring until dissolved, then add the lemon juice and bring to the boil. Boil rapidly until setting point is reached. Pour into warm, sterilised jars, cover with waxed discs and seal.

Chestnut Jam

This old country recipe is for an unusual preserve which is not seen much nowadays.

2 lbs chestnuts   1½ lbs sugar
1 vanilla pod

Slit the chestnut shells (to prevent them exploding in the oven) and place on a baking tray or in a roasting tin and put into a hot oven, 400°F or Mark 6, for 15-20 minutes; alternatively place the slit nuts on a plate, six at a time, in the microwave and microwave for 30-60 seconds. Peel the nuts whilst hot, to ensure removal of the inner brown furry skin, which is bitter. Place the peeled chestnuts in a pan and cover with cold water. Bring to the boil and cook for 30-40 minutes until tender. Drain and rub through a sieve to purée. Add the sugar to the warm purée and place in a pan with 3 tablespoons water per lb of sweetened purée. Add the vanilla pod and place over a low heat, stirring all the time. Cook until the mixture is stiff and comes away from the base of the pan. Remove from the heat and take out the vanilla pod. Spoon into warm, sterilised jars and cover with waxed discs and lids. Store in a cool dry place.

Dumpsie Dearie Jam

An old country recipe from Gloucestershire which makes use of windfall apples, pears and plums.

2 lbs pears	**Grated zest and juice of 1 lemon**
2 lbs cooking apples	**Pinch ground cloves**
2 lbs plums	**½ oz fresh ginger root, bruised**
5 lbs sugar	

Peel and core the pears and apples. Halve and stone the plums. Put all the fruit into a large pan with the lemon zest and juice, the ground cloves and bruised ginger root. Simmer very gently until the fruit is soft; if it starts to stick to the pan add a little water. Stir in the sugar until completely dissolved and then bring to the boil. Boil rapidly for about 15-20 minutes until setting point is reached. Pour into warm, sterilised jars, cover and seal.

Rose Petal Jam

A sweet jam with a delicate, scented flavour. Use heavily perfumed rose petals,
for example damask, and make sure they have not been sprayed with insecticide.

½ lb rose petals	4 tablespoons water
½ lb sugar	1 dessertspoon orange juice
1 dessertspoon lemon juice	

Remove the white 'heel' at the base of the petals, as this is bitter tasting. Place the petals in a pan and add the sugar, water and juices. Place over a very low heat until the sugar has dissolved. Bring to the boil and boil rapidly until setting point is reached. Cool slightly before pouring into warm, sterilised jars and cover and seal immediately.

Uncooked Raspberry Jam

All the wonderful flavour of fresh raspberries is preserved in this easy-to-make jam which is stored in the freezer. Strawberries can also be used in this way.

2 lbs raspberries   Juice of 1 lemon
1 lb sugar with pectin (jam sugar)

Place the raspberries in a non-metallic bowl and crush them with a wooden spoon. Stir in the sugar, cover the bowl and put into the oven, set at the lowest setting, until warm, but do not allow to become hot. Remove from the oven and leave to stand for 1 hour, stirring now and again until the sugar has dissolved. Stir in the lemon juice. Pack the mixture into small, freezer-proof containers, leaving plenty of room for expansion. Cover and seal and leave at room temperature for 6 hours. Place in the refrigerator to chill for 1-2 days until jellied. Store in the freezer and thaw for 1 hour to serve. Once thawed the jam will keep in the refrigerator for 2-3 days.

Medlar Jelly

*Medlars are brown, golf ball size fruits with hard, rough skin. The flavour is lightly
spicy and rather tart. After picking, the fruit must be allowed to 'blett'; that is
become soft and brown inside. A native English fruit, they can sometimes
be found growing wild in the countryside.*

**4 lbs medlars   3 pints water
1 large lemon   Sugar (see recipe)**

Wash and chop the medlars and put into a large pan with sufficient water to cover
the fruit. Simmer slowly until the fruit is reduced to a brown pulp. Strain through
a scalded jelly bag, then measure the juice and return to the pan. For every 1 pint
juice weigh out 12 oz sugar. Put the sugar in a bowl and place in a very cool oven,
225°F or Mark ¼, until warm and dry. Add the lemon juice to the juice in the pan
and bring to the boil. Stir in the warmed sugar and stir, without boiling, until the
sugar has dissolved. Increase the heat and boil rapidly until setting point is reached
(about 25 minutes). Skim off any scum with a metal spoon and pour into warm,
sterilised jars immediately, before the jelly sets. Cover with waxed discs and leave
until cold before sealing with a lid or cellophane cover.

Quince Jelly

Quinces are inedible when raw, but have a delightful flavour when cooked. The raw fruit is very hard, with a yellowish-green skin which is covered with down. The flesh turns deep pink when cooked. As this jelly cooks it will fill the house with a wonderful perfume. Add a spoonful of quince jelly to apple pies or crumbles before cooking or serve with roast meats and game.

4 lbs quinces   6 pints water
Sugar (see recipe)

Wash the quinces and rub away the grey down. Chop the fruit roughly and place in a large pan with 5 pints water. Cover and simmer over a low heat until soft; about an hour, depending on the ripeness of the fruit. When soft, press the fruit with the back of a wooden spoon. Ladle the fruit and juice into a scalded jelly bag and leave to drip for 30 minutes. Remove the pulp from the bag and return to the pan with the remaining water. Simmer for 30 minutes, then ladle back into the jelly bag for a second straining. Measure all the juice into the rinsed out pan and for every 1 pint juice add 1 lb granulated sugar. Cook over a low heat, stirring, until the sugar has dissolved, then bring to the boil and boil rapidly until setting point is reached (about 10 minutes). Skim off any scum with a metal spoon and pour into warm, sterilised jars. Cover with waxed discs and leave to become cold before sealing.

Parsley Honey

During the Second World War, when honey was very difficult to obtain, this was a popular substitute for the real thing. It looks and tastes like heather honey.

6 oz fresh parsley   1½ pints water   1 lb sugar, approx.
½ teaspoon vinegar or juice of 1 small lemon

Wash the parsley well and dry thoroughly. Chop it roughly, including the stalks and put into a pan with the water. Bring to the boil and simmer gently for 30 minutes. Strain through a jelly bag and measure the resulting juice. Put the juice into a clean pan with the vinegar or lemon juice and 1 lb sugar for every 1 pint parsley juice. Stir well over a low heat until the sugar has dissolved, then bring to the boil. Reduce the heat and simmer gently for 30 minutes or so, until the mixture is clear and syrupy, like thin honey. Pour into warm, sterilised jars and cover and seal while hot.

Lemon Curd

Home-made lemon curd tastes so much nicer than the commercial variety, and it has a lovely fresh, tangy flavour.

Grated zest and juice of 2 large lemons
6 oz caster sugar   4 large eggs   4 oz unsalted butter, diced

Combine the lemon zest and sugar in a mixing bowl. In another bowl beat the eggs well with the lemon juice and pour into the lemon zest and sugar.   Add the butter and place the bowl over a pan of hot (not boiling) water and cook very gently, stirring until thick; about 20 minutes. Pour into warm, sterilised jars and cover with waxed discs and seal. Store in a cool place and use within a month.

Strawberry and Orange Curd

This spread is an ideal way of using up the last of the summer strawberries which may be over ripe or squashed.

8 oz strawberries, hulled **4 oz unsalted butter, diced**
Grated zest and juice of 1 orange **12 oz caster sugar**
4 eggs, beaten

Place the strawberries in a bowl and mash with a fork. Stir in the orange zest and juice, butter and sugar. Beat the eggs and add to the mixture. Place the bowl over a pan of simmering water and stir until the sugar has dissolved. Continue to cook until the mixture thickens, stirring frequently; about 30 minutes. Pour into warm, sterilised jars and cover with waxed discs and seal with lids or cellophane covers. Label and store in the refrigerator.

Apricot Curd

*Golden juicy apricots make a toothsome spread for fresh bread and butter and scones.
Add a few of the cracked stones to the mixture for a subtle almond flavour; but
remember to remove them before potting.*

8 oz fresh apricots	**8 oz caster sugar**
Grated zest and juice of 1 lemon	**Water**
1½ oz butter, diced	**2 eggs, beaten**

Wash the fruit and put into a pan with very little water and cook until soft. Push the mixture through a nylon sieve into a heat-proof bowl and stir in the sugar, lemon zest and juice and the butter. Place the bowl over a pan of hot (not boiling) water and cook, stirring, until the sugar has dissolved. Add the eggs and continue to cook until thick. Pour into warm, sterilised jars and cover with waxed discs and lids or cellophane covers. Label and store in a cool place.

Quince Butter

Simple to make and ideal if only a few quinces are available. This spread can be eaten with bread and butter or as an accompaniment to roast pork.

Quinces	**Sugar (see recipe)**
Water	**Knob of butter**

Wash the quinces and rub away the grey down. Cut the fruit into quite small pieces and place in a pan with a little water. Cook until the fruit is soft and can be rubbed through a sieve. After sieving, measure the pulp by volume and add three-quarters of its volume of sugar and the knob of butter. Cook over a low heat, stirring all the time until thick; the mixture tends to stick to the pan and burn if not stirred constantly. Remove any scum from the surface and spoon into warm, sterilised jars. Cover with plastic or metal lids immediately.

Blackberry Butter

A beautiful, deep coloured spread which is equally delicious with scones and cream or as a filling for a sponge cake. A good way of using up the results of a late summer blackberrying expedition!

2 lbs blackberries   **Grated zest and juice of 2 lemons**
2 lbs cooking apples   **12 oz sugar to every 1 lb fruit pulp**

Wash the fruit and chop the apples roughly; there is no need to core and peel them. Place in a pan with the lemon zest and juice and simmer gently for about 15 minutes until very soft. Rub through a sieve and weigh the pulp. Stir in the required amount of sugar and heat gently until the sugar has dissolved completely. Bring to the boil and cook gently until the mixture is thick and creamy, stirring all the time; about 20 minutes, depending on the ripeness of the fruit. Pour into warm, sterilised jars and cover with plastic or metal lids.

Chutneys and Pickles

Chutneys originated in India and the name comes from the word "Chatni", meaning a strong, sweet relish. They first appeared in Britain in the seventeenth century. Pickling is an ancient method of preserving fruits and vegetables in season and has been used in Britain since Roman times. Fruit and vegetables used for pickling must be fresh and free from blemishes. Choose a good quality pickling vinegar. Always use a stainless steel or aluminium pan for chutneys and pickles. Never use brass, copper or iron utensils as vinegar will corrode these metals. Chutneys are usually cooked very slowly for a long time to give a rich, mellow flavour and a dark colour. To test when chutney is cooked, make a channel across the surface in the pan with a wooden spoon. If the impression lasts for a few seconds and does not fill up with vinegar, then the chutney is ready. When ready, pour the hot chutney into warmed jars right up to the brim and cover while still hot. Use plastic-lined lids as vinegar corrodes metal. Chutney will taste better if left to mature for at least three months, and will keep in a cool, dry, dark place for 2-3 years. Pickles will keep similarly for a year.

Orange and Lemon Chutney

This chutney has a refreshing taste which goes well with duck, goose or ham.

2 oranges, scrubbed	**Piece fresh root ginger, bruised**
3 lemons, scrubbed	**1 teaspoon whole cloves**
1 lb cooking apples	**1 blade mace**
¾ pint white wine vinegar	**8 oz onions, finely chopped**
1 cinnamon stick	**6 oz sultanas**
A few peppercorns	**1 lb sugar**

Salt and pepper to taste

Halve the oranges and lemons and squeeze the juices into a bowl. Finely shred the peel and flesh and discard the pips. Put the juice, shredded peel and flesh into a large bowl and add the vinegar and spices. Stir well, cover and leave to stand for 24 hours. Next day, place the mixture in a large pan. Peel, core and chop the apples and add to the pan with the onions. Cook very gently until the fruit and vegetables are tender. Remove from the heat and stir in the sultanas and sugar and season with salt and pepper to taste. When the sugar has completely dissolved, return to the heat and bring to the boil. Reduce the heat and simmer gently for about an hour until the mixture is thick and the vinegar absorbed (see note on testing). Pour into warm, sterilised jars and seal immediately.

Elderberry Chutney

A surprising chutney with a wonderful fruity flavour. Glossy, black elderberries can be found growing wild in the autumn. The easiest way to remove the berries from the stalks is to strip them using the prongs of a fork.

1 lb elderberries, washed and stalks removed	**1 teaspoon salt**
1 lb cooking apples	**½ teaspoon ground ginger**
4 oz dried fruit, e.g. currants, sultanas, raisins	**½ teaspoon ground mixed spice**
	Pinch of pepper
8 oz onions, finely chopped	**½ pint malt vinegar**
	12 oz soft brown sugar

Peel, core and chop the apples and put into a large pan with the elderberries, raisins and onions. Stir in the salt, spices and pepper and a little of the vinegar. Cook very gently for 1 hour until the fruit is soft, stirring from time to time to prevent the mixture sticking and burning. Remove from the heat and stir in the sugar and remaining vinegar. When the sugar has dissolved completely, return to the heat and bring to the boil. Boil steadily for about 30-40 minutes until thick and all the vinegar is absorbed (see note on testing). Spoon into warm, sterilised jars and seal immediately.

Uncooked Chutney

A simple recipe, is ready to eat as soon as it is made. It will keep for up to 6 weeks.

8 oz dates, finely chopped　　　**½ pint malt vinegar**
8 oz apples, peeled and chopped　**1 teaspoon salt**
8 oz sultanas and raisins, mixed　**Pinch each of mustard powder**
8 oz onion, finely chopped　　　　**and ground pepper**
8 oz dark soft brown sugar　　　　**¼ teaspoon ground cinnamon**
Pince of ground cloves

Mix all the ingredients together, very well, in a large bowl. Spoon into cold, sterilised jars, filling to the brim. Seal and store in a cool, dry place.

Green Tomato Chutney

A recipe that was popular with the Victorians, who regarded this as an ideal accompaniment to cheeses and cold meats.

4 lbs green tomatoes, sliced	**½ oz fresh root ginger, bruised**
1 lb cooking apples	**1 lb soft brown sugar**
1¼ lbs shallots or onions	**1 teaspoon salt**
2 cloves garlic (optional)	**½ teaspoon cayenne pepper**
8 oz raisins	**1 pint vinegar**

Peel, core and chop the apples. Peel and finely chop the shallots or onions and garlic. Place the tomatoes, apples, shallots or onions, garlic and raisins in a large pan with the salt and cayenne pepper. Tie the ginger loosely in a piece of muslin and add to the pan. Stir in a little of the vinegar and cook gently over a low heat for about an hour until the vegetable and fruit are soft, stirring from time to time. Remove from the heat and stir in the sugar and remaining vinegar. When the sugar has dissolved completely, return to the heat and bring to the boil. Cook gently for 1-1½ hours until thick and the vinegar is absorbed (see note on testing). Pour into warm, sterilised jars and seal immediately.

Lavender Chutney

An unusual, spicy chutney made with fresh lavender flowers, which goes well with cold meats and cheeses. Be sure to use blooms free from insecticide. Shake the flowers gently to dislodge any insects and wash very gently in cold water. Dry the flowers on kitchen paper immediately after washing, to preserve the fragrance.

20 lavender flowers, chopped
2 tablespoons mustard seeds
3 lemons, scrubbed and chopped
Salt
3 onions, finely chopped

2 oz sultanas
1 cinnamon stick
Pinch ground allspice
Sugar to taste
White wine vinegar

Chop the lemons into small pieces, remove the pith and the pips. Place in a mixing bowl and sprinkle with salt. Pour in enough vinegar to cover the lemons and cover the bowl. Leave to stand for 24 hours. Next day, place the mixture in a large pan and add the rest of the ingredients, stirring until the sugar has dissolved. Bring to the boil, then reduce the heat and simmer gently until the mixture is thick and the vinegar absorbed (see note on testing). Remove the cinnamon stick and pour into warm, sterilised jars and seal tightly.

Mango Chutney

The traditional accompaniment to curries. The recipe is said to have been given to an English lady in Bengal in the nineteenth century. If mangoes are unobtainable, tangerines or plums can be used instead.

2½ lbs mangoes, peeled, halved and stoned
1 oz salt
1 pint white wine vinegar
2 inch piece fresh root ginger, peeled and grated

8 oz soft brown sugar
2½ oz raisins
4 oz dates, finely chopped
1 cinnamon stick
¼ teaspoon cayenne pepper
½ teaspoon grated nutmeg

Chop the mangoes into small pieces and lay them in a shallow dish. Sprinkle with a little of the salt, cover with a clean cloth and leave for 24 hours. Next day, drain well in a colander. Place the sugar and vinegar in a large pan and bring to the boil. Add the drained mangoes and the remaining ingredients and bring back to the boil, stirring occasionally. Cook gently, uncovered, for 1¼-1½ hours until thick and the vinegar is absorbed (see note on testing). Discard the cinnamon stick and ladle into warm, sterilised jars. Seal at once.

Piccalilli

The recipe for 'Sweet Indian Pickle' was brought to England from the East in the seventeenth century. It is delicious with cold meats and cheeses. Use a mixture of cauliflower, cucumber, green beans, green tomatoes, pickling onions and marrow.

3 lbs prepared vegetables	**1 oz flour**
8 oz salt	**1 tablespoon mustard powder**
3½ pints water	**2 teaspoons turmeric**
4 oz Demerara sugar	**1 teaspoon ground ginger**
1½ pints distilled white vinegar	

Cut all the vegetables into small even-sized pieces and place in a large bowl. Dissolve the salt in the water and pour over the vegetables. Keep the vegetables submerged with a weighted plate and cover the bowl with a cloth. Leave to stand for 24 hours then drain the vegetables and rinse thoroughly. Place the vegetables in a large pan with the sugar, spices and most of the vinegar and simmer gently until they are as crisp or as tender as preferred. Remove the vegetables with a perforated spoon and put into hot, sterilised jars. Mix the flour, turmeric and mustard with the remaining vinegar and stir into the hot liquid in the pan. Bring to the boil and boil for 1 minute then pour over the vegetables. Gently tap the jars on a work surface to remove any air bubbles and top up with more sauce if necessary. Cover and seal while hot and store for 3 months before using.

Spiced Pickled Pears

In the days when fruit was available only when in season, fruits were often preserved in this way. These pears can be served with any cold meats or poultry. Apples or quinces can be used instead of pears if preferred.

3 lbs cooking pears	**½ teaspoon grated nutmeg**
Slightly salted cold water	**1 teaspoon ground cinnamon**
1 pint distilled white vinegar	**1 lb granulated sugar**
1 teaspoon ground mixed spice	**Peel of ½ lemon**

Peel, halve (or quarter) and core the pears and put into slightly salted water to prevent them becoming brown. Mix a little of the vinegar with the spices and put the remaining vinegar and the sugar into a pan with the lemon rind. Heat gently until the sugar has dissolved completely, then add the spice mixture and bring to the boil. Rinse the pears and add to the pan. Simmer gently until the pears look clear and are tender, but not broken. Remove the pears, using a perforated spoon and put into warm, sterilised jars. Discard the lemon peel and boil the liquid until it has thickened to a syrup. Pour over the pears to cover them completely and seal the jars immediately.

Ladies Delight

This old Shropshire pickle recipe is especially tasty spread on cold roast beef sandwiches or served alongside pork pies or sausages. Wear rubber gloves when deseeding and chopping the chillies.

8 oz apples	**1½-2 oz chillies**
8 oz onions, finely chopped	**1 pint white distilled vinegar**
2 oz sultanas or raisins	**1 tablespoon cooking salt**

Peel, core and chop the apples and mix with the onions and sultanas. Discard the seeds from the chillies and chop finely. Add to the apple mixture in the bowl. Place the vinegar and salt in a pan and heat until boiling. Pour over the ingredients and mix well. Cover and leave until completely cold, then spoon into cold, sterilised jars and seal.

Spiced Orange Slices

These are expensive to buy in food stores, but are not difficult to make at home.
They make a tasty accompaniment to ham, roast duck or pork.

6 oranges	**8 cloves**
½ pint distilled white vinegar	**1 cinnamon stick**
1 lb granulated sugar	**1 teaspoon allspice berries**

Cut the fruit into $\frac{1}{8}$ - $\frac{3}{16}$ inch slices and discard the pips. Put the orange slices into a pan and pour over just enough cold water to cover. Bring to the boil, then reduce the heat and simmer gently for 1 hour, until the peel is tender. Remove the oranges to a bowl with a perforated spoon. Put the vinegar, sugar and spices into a pan and heat gently until the sugar has dissolved completely. Bring to the boil and add the orange slices, then reduce the heat and simmer gently for about $\frac{1}{2}$ hour until the orange slices appear glazed. Remove from the heat and discard the cinnamon stick. Using a perforated spoon, put the oranges and remaining spices into warm sterilised jars. Return the pan to the heat and boil rapidly for 10 minutes to reduce the liquid and concentrate the flavour. Pour over the fruit in the jars; there should be enough to cover the orange slices. Cover tightly with vinegar-proof lids when cold.

Pickled Plums

These are delicious with cold game pies as well as any cold meats and poultry.
Small red plums, damsons or greengages can be used in this recipe.

1 lb small plums
½ pint distilled white vinegar
8 oz sugar
Rind of ½ lemon

Small piece fresh root ginger,
bruised
4 whole cloves
1 cinnamon stick

Wash and dry the plums and remove the stalks. Prick the fruit all over with a darning needle and place in a pan. Cover with vinegar and add the sugar. Tie the lemon rind and the spices in a piece of muslin and add to the pan. Heat gently, stirring, until the sugar has dissolved completely, then bring to the boil. Reduce the heat and simmer very gently until the fruit is tender, but do not let the skins break. Remove the fruit with a perforated spoon and pack into warm, sterilised jars. Discard the muslin and boil the liquid rapidly for 5 minutes then pour immediately over the plums and cover the jars at once. Keep for at least 1 month before eating.

Marmalades and Mincemeat

Marmalade was originally a medieval confection made from quinces. The first proper orange marmalade was made from bitter Seville oranges by the Keiller family of Dundee in the 18th century. Marmalade is made in the same way as jam, but needs a longer cooking time. Scrub the fruit well to remove any waxy coating or fungicide. The pectin which gives the set is mainly in the pith and pips, so these must be kept, tied loosely in a piece of muslin and added to the pan. The secret of good marmalade is fast boiling. Test after 15 minutes then every 5 minutes, in the same way as for jam. When setting point is reached, remove from the heat and let the mixture stand for 10-20 minutes, when a skin will form. This cooling prevents the peel rising after potting. Stir once before pouring into the jars and the peel will be suspended evenly in the jelly.

Mincemeat was first recorded in the 16th century and contained a substantial quantity of minced meat with dried fruits and spices. Later the recipe acquired alcohol. Today the only meat in the recipe is the suet, and now there is the option of using vegetable suet. There is also here a recipe for mincemeat without any suet, for those who like a rich, fatless mincemeat. All mincemeat will keep for a year in a dry, cool place so long as enough spirit is added to preserve the ingredients.

Rum and Raisin Marmalade

This recipe makes a delicious change from marmalade made solely from citrus fruits.
As it contains alcohol it is unsuitable for children. Use it to make tasty puddings,
tarts and ice cream. The almonds can be omitted, if preferred.

1½ lbs sweet oranges, thinly sliced   **6 oz raisins**
1½ lbs lemons, thinly sliced   **6 lbs sugar, warmed in a very low oven**
3 pints water   **8 dessertspoons rum**
1 oz almonds, chopped

Place the sliced fruit into a large pan with the water and raisins and bring to the boil. Simmer gently for 1½-2 hours until the peel is very tender. Stir in the warm sugar until it has dissolved completely then boil rapidly until setting point is reached. Remove from the heat and allow to stand for 10-20 minutes. Stir in the almonds and rum and pour into warm sterilised jars. Cover immediately with waxed discs and seal when cold.

Orange and Ginger Marmalade

Either stem ginger (from a jar) or crystallised ginger can be used in this recipe.
The combination of flavours produces a warm, spicy marmalade.

2 lbs Seville oranges, scrubbed	5 pints water
2 lemons, scrubbed	6 lbs sugar, warmed in a very low oven
1 oz fresh root ginger	8 oz stem or crystallised ginger, chopped

Halve the oranges and lemons and squeeze out the juice and pips. Remove any thick white pith and chop this roughly. Peel and chop the root ginger and tie loosely in a piece of muslin with the pips, pith and orange flesh. Place the muslin in a large pan with the orange and lemon juices. Cut the orange and lemon peel into fine shreds and add to the pan with the water. Bring to the boil, then reduce the heat and simmer for 1½-2 hours until the peel is tender. Squeeze the muslin bag juices into the pan and discard. Stir in the warm sugar, over a low heat, until completely dissolved and add the chopped ginger. Boil rapidly until setting point is reached. Remove from the heat and leave to stand for 10-20 minutes. Stir well to disperse the ginger and pour into warm, sterilised jars. Cover with waxed discs and seal when cold.

Grapefruit and Lemon Marmalade

*Made from two tart, refreshing citrus fruits, this marmalade has a
wonderful fruity flavour.*

2 lbs grapefruit, scrubbed   **6 pints water**
1 lb lemons, scrubbed   **6 lbs sugar, warmed in a very low oven**

Place the fruit in boiling water for 3 minutes; this makes the fruit easier to peel.
Remove from the water and peel with a potato peeler. Cut the peel into fine shreds
and place in a large pan. Remove the pith from the fruit and chop the flesh roughly.
Add the flesh to the pan together with any juice from the fruit. Place the pith and
pips in a muslin bag and add to the pan with the water. Bring to the boil, then
simmer gently for 1-1½ hours until the peel is tender. Squeeze out any juice from
the muslin bag into the pan and discard. Stir in the warm sugar and heat gently until
completely dissolved. Increase the heat and boil rapidly until setting point is
reached. Remove from the heat and leave to stand for 10-20 minutes before pouring
into warm, sterilised jars. Cover with waxed discs and seal when cold.

Mincemeat without Suet

This recipe is made with cider and glacé cherries and produces a rich tasting mincemeat with a difference.

¾ **pint medium cider**
1 lb soft dark brown sugar
4 lbs cooking apples, peeled,
   cored and chopped
1 teaspoon ground mixed spice
1 teaspoon ground cinnamon

Pinch of ground cloves
1 lb currants
1 lb raisins
4 oz glacé cherries, chopped
4 oz almonds, finely chopped
Grated zest and juice of 1 lemon

¼ **pint brandy or rum**

Put the cider and sugar into a large pan and heat gently until the sugar has completely dissolved. Stir in the rest of the ingredients, except the brandy or rum and slowly bring to the boil, stirring all the time. Lower the heat, partially cover the pan and simmer for 30 minutes. Remove from the heat and leave to become completely cold. Stir in the brandy or rum and spoon into cold, sterilised jars making sure there are no air bubbles. Cover with waxed discs and tight fitting lids.

Traditional Mincemeat

Home-made mincemeat is much superior to shop bought and is easy to make. It is best made one to three months before using, to allow the flavours to develop. It is desirable to buy whole candied peel and chop it, as the flavour is much nicer than the rather bitter peel sold ready diced in tubs.

1 lb cooking apples, cored and chopped, but unpeeled
8 oz shredded suet
12 oz raisins
8 oz currants
8 oz sultanas
4 oz candied orange peel
4 oz candied lemon peel

4 oz slivered almonds
Grated zest and juice of 1 lemon
12 oz soft dark brown sugar
2 heaped teaspoons mixed ground spice
½ teaspoon grated nutmeg
½ teaspoon ground cinnamon
½ teaspoon ground ginger
7 tablespoons brandy

Mix all the ingredients, except the brandy, in a large heat-proof bowl, stirring well until thoroughly combined. Cover the bowl and leave overnight for the flavours to blend. Next day, stir the ingredients well and cover with foil. Place in a very cool oven, 225°F or Mark ¼, for 3 hours. Remove from the oven and leave to cool, stirring occasionally until all the ingredients are coated in the melted suet. When the mixture is completely cold, stir in the brandy. Pack into cold, sterilised jars, making sure there are no air bubbles. Cover with waxed discs and seal with lids.

cottage gate; Springtime

Russet Mincemeat

This is an old country recipe for an unusual but delectable mincemeat.

8 oz shredded suet
8 oz dried apricots, chopped
8 oz cooking apples, peeled,
  cored and chopped
8 oz prunes, stoned and chopped
8 oz sultanas
4 oz glacé cherries, chopped

4 oz candied peel, finely diced
2 oz almonds, chopped
1 tablespoon honey
1 teaspoon ground cinnamon
Large pinch ground cloves
Grated zest and juice of 1 lemon
Grated zest and juice of 1 orange

1 pint ginger wine

Combine all the ingredients in a large mixing bowl, stirring very well. Cover and leave to stand overnight to allow the flavours to blend. Next day, spoon into cold sterilised jars making sure there are no air bubbles, cover with waxed discs and then with tight fitting plastic or metal lids.

Apricot and Almond Mincemeat

A recipe for those who dislike the taste of traditional mincemeat. Hazelnuts or walnuts can be substituted for the almonds if preferred.

1 lb cooking apples, peeled, cored and chopped
8 oz raisins
8 oz figs, finely chopped
1 lb dried apricots, finely chopped
1 lb sultanas
4 oz glacé cherries, chopped
4 oz almonds, chopped

2 oz crystallised ginger, finely chopped
8 oz shredded suet
12 oz soft brown sugar
Grated zest and juice of 1 lemon
Grated zest and juice of 1 orange
1 teaspoon ground mixed spice
1 teaspoon ground cinnamon
¼ pint rum or brandy

Combine all the ingredients in a large bowl, stirring very well. Cover the bowl and leave to stand overnight. Next day, stir the mixture thoroughly to combine the ingredients and spoon into cold, sterilised jars, making sure there are no air bubbles. Cover with waxed discs and tight fitting lids.

METRIC CONVERSIONS

The weights, measures and oven temperatures used in the preceding recipes can be easily converted to their metric equivalents. The conversions listed below are only approximate, having been rounded up or down as may be appropriate.

Weights

Avoirdupois	Metric
1 oz.	just under 30 grams
4 oz. (¼ lb.)	app. 115 grams
8 oz. (½ lb.)	app. 230 grams
1 lb.	454 grams

Liquid Measures

Imperial	Metric
1 tablespoon (liquid only)	20 millilitres
1 fl. oz.	app. 30 millilitres
1 gill (¼ pt.)	app. 145 millilitres
½ pt.	app. 285 millilitres
1 pt.	app. 570 millilitres
1 qt.	app. 1.140 litres

Oven Temperatures

	°Fahrenheit	Gas Mark	°Celsius
Slow	300	2	150
	325	3	170
Moderate	350	4	180
	375	5	190
	400	6	200
Hot	425	7	220
	450	8	230
	475	9	240

Flour as specified in these recipes refers to Plain flour unless otherwise described.